TESTAMENT · DENNIS LEE

ALSO BY DENNIS LEE

Kingdom of Absence · 1967
Civil Elegies · 1968, 1972
The Death of Harold Ladoo · 1976
Savage Fields: An Essay in Literature and Cosmology · 1977
The Gods · 1979
Riffs · 1993
Nightwatch: New and Selected Poems · 1996
Body Music · 1998
Un · 2003
Yesno · 2007
The Bard of the Universe · 2007

for Children

Wiggle to the Laundromat · 1970
Alligator Pie · 1974
Nicholas Knock and Other People · 1974
Garbage Delight · 1977, 2002
The Ordinary Bath · 1979
Jelly Belly · 1983
Lizzy's Lion · 1984
The Difficulty of Living on Other Planets · 1987
The Ice Cream Store · 1991
Dinosaur Dinner · 1997
Bubblegum Delicious · 2000
The Cat and the Wizard · 2001
SoCool · 2004

DENNIS LEE

testament

ANANSI

House of Anansi Press Inc.
110 Spadina Avenue, Suite 801
Toronto, ON M5V 2K4
Tel. 416-363-4343
Fax 416-363-1017
www.houseofanansi.com

Distributed in Canada by
HarperCollins Canada Ltd.
1995 Markham Road
Scarborough, ON M1B 5M8
Toll free tel. 1-800-387-0117

House of Anansi Press is committed to protecting our natural environment. As part of our efforts, this book is printed on paper that contains 100% post-consumer recycled fibres, is acid-free, and is processed chlorine-free.

16 15 14 13 12 2 3 4 5 6

MIX
Paper from
responsible sources
FSC® C004071

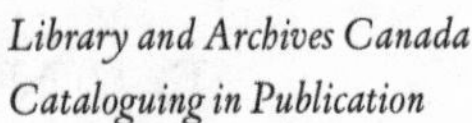

Library and Archives Canada Cataloguing in Publication

Lee, Dennis, 1939–
Testament : poems / Dennis Lee.

ISBN 978-0-88784-758-5

I. Title.

PS8523.E3Y48 2007   C811'.54
C2007-900068-1

Canada Council for the Arts   Conseil des Arts du Canada

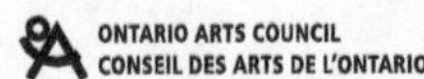

We acknowledge for their financial support of our publishing program the Canada Council for the Arts, the Ontario Arts Council, and the Government of Canada through the Canada Book Fund.

Printed and bound in Canada.

CONTENTS

UN

3 *blues*

I

7 inwreck
8 rupture
9 slub
10 brainrays
11 hydro
12 shotgut
13 slipaway
14 pidgin
15 *tap*
16 mayday

II

19 genesis
20 olduvai
21 toxibelle
22 names
23 unsaying
24 scarlight
25 lascaux
26 admire
27 tagalong
28 grief

III

31 tame
32 bears
33 inlingo
34 hang-
35 innerly
36 ologies
37 beloved
38 *yip*
39 goodbye
40 excalibur

IV

43 exodus
44 history
45 hiatus
46 ancel
47 trump
48 *familia*
49 lungfast
50 *desaparecidos*
51 nozone
52 home

V

55 word
56 noth
57 trolling
58 befalse
59 wordward
60 *floruit*
61 youwho
62 lullabye
63 blind
64 stone

YESNO

67 *song*

VI

71 apocalypse
72 blah-
73 *awk*
74 bwana
75 hope
76 ganglia
77 still
78 chumps
79 holdon
80 noful

VII

83 tarbaby
84 bambino
85 asif
86 *boom!*
87 whistledown
88 oompah
89 *ave*
90 *oomph*
91 twin
92 DNA

VIII

95 whatcan
96 googoo
97 biscript
98 larrup
99 avian
100 amigos
101 pinsteps
102 flux
103 tango
105 [ ]

IX

109 back
110 fold
111 listen
112 diggity
113 BANG
114 quick
115 bandwidth
116 stinct
117 *forgi-*
118 survive

X

121 *abc*
122 tilth
123 extemp
124 dopey
125 *yesno*
126 demesne
127 mutt
128 galore
129 orwhat
130 tale

UN

A little planet blues, for the
deathwatch.
A season of rictus riffs.
(When schist prevails, and squamous
pinpricks of appetite
vamp to a second future – who'll chant the
mutant genesis? who celebrate
an aevum cleansed of us?)

I

In wreck, in dearth, in necksong,
godnexus gone to fat of the land,
into the wordy desyllabification of evil – small
crawlspace for plegics, 4, 3, 2, 1, un.

Mind, and a home, and a rupture:
old mother mutanda.
Surd journeys to scrambled states of once.
Lymphflange and cowsprocket; neurotectonics; organs.com.
Contusions of slippage & sloppage & inconsolable
us, re-
formatted to the new.

I want verbs of a slagscape thrombosis.
Syntax of chromosome pileups.
Make me
slubtalk; gerundibles; gummy embouchure.

Icecaps shrink in the brainrays.
Leaf protocols gone skewy, mind-to-
green ratios a
barbous disproportion.
Synapse events on the pampas, while
consciousness voids all over the bowl of sky.

New signatures of loss.
Fresh spoor of extinctions.
Late atmo of
warmfront & hazmat *bup-bupp*ing.
Coastal was comfort but soon a new swaddle of no-go.
Oceans placental, but soon a new hydro of gone.

Shotgut and
starways. Liturgy
offal. Residue eyes. Down
down down in the
belly of, dank in the relict, un-
winkled & dree.
Taxiderm inklings of mineral mind in extremis.
Clubfoot hosannas. Exfoliate consonant prod.

Of the metrophysics of ice:
slip away, seaboard.
In Greenland, a glacial divide – and
last call for littoral cities,
slipaway Sydney.
London.   Manhattan.   Mumbai:
nostril meniscus, then ciao.
Or dykage, and stiltage, and humanoid critters
vying with dogfish for allsorts.   Slip-
slipaway Athens, Rangoon, sub-
aqueous fables of *was.*
Rio.   Vancouver.   Shanghai –
slipslipaway Buenos Aires.

Cumuloss rising.   History slop in the wash.

Scribblescript portents unfurl, world-
to, worldfro.
And to comb the signs, to
stammer the uterine painscape
in pidgin apocalypse – how now not
gag on the unward, the once-upon, us-
proud planet?

Tap-tap the embryo spooks at the portals of ego.
Gone-boy the party-hard hoots from the house of condamned.
Too-tardy heroes, marching to/marching to drumbelow.
Misters of techabye fixit, where did the world go?

Snoozing to mayday – the
eyes in the headlights are us.
How long till
brakeback skid? till
autowhammy meltdown? How soon till nocan-
wannavamoose?

II

Under the cloak of day, heroic
mutations.
Out of the is-
scape, the iffy human smear.
Anthropox rising. Eschatosclerotic rose.

In gabbro, in arcady vitro,
hellbright ego.
In Olduvai, fester and eros.
And the teleo-
skookum surge to hominid dominion: what geocidal
grandeur? what germinal terminus schuss?

Toxibelle, mon
fleur de ciao:
rose of dis-
owning, you open in
ozone in shoah in nofold embryonics.
Lady of nichtlichkeit, you flower somatic, en-
tropic, dyschthonic, till
no thing is proof.

That the names will end, that the
naming will end, that
the undis-
claimable forceducts of *is* will
resume their
eddies of post and pre.

Disarticulations of the stilled will,
I hear you inching.
Syllabic unhitchings among the galactic nevermind.
Expats of the pax humana; susurration of
fingerless glyphs in the limbo.

And speak athwart the scrutable.
Grain of un-
saying, and how.
Past lingolock pitons, reopening
forte and stillshine: that
hail of, that howl of unmuzzled desire.

Scarlight, scar-
blight in the chronifrag of no-man's:
sublingual agon.
Rolled scarlight up the hill, got
crushed, rolled
scarlight up the hill.

Of palaeopresence. The extra
space around what is.

Is – now
there was a word. Was
funnelforce eddy of
strut & incumbence; pelt
yenful; carnivorous abc-meat.   Walls
juiced with kinetic copula – now
shrunk to a nominal gloss.
(Who combed the wind with horses,
who grazed with aurochs;
who champed in co-domain.)

Totting this
boulder, that cedar, this
street that square, tick by
tock by admire: to
be is a bare-assed wonder, and in the
lethal occasions of earth it hunkers blessed.

Tagalong
snatches, algorithmic
hums. You even wear gene
disguises. Little anti-
threnodic peeps, tell nix in the slurry:
some-
thing matters, no
matter how nano the known.

Earth in the end days:
I gave good
grief. How-
ever you knew me, a bible a babel a-
merican bauble,
thru plague & renewals by
cullkill & mitzvah and
on-again/green-again/gone-again always I
gave good grief.

Carbon to kittiwake, lava to gita
I gave good grief.

III

How cleave to the skank of extincting? How
signify unday?
We named it, we tamed it, we
gutted & framed it – and
thar she be: clean-clean, with a soupçon of *tsk-tsk*.

Me dork among parsewords.   Me dis in the lexic.
My beat, subsyl-
labic inferno.

The one about the bears.
What oncely
meant, corona:
starlight star-
bright star
kucked & cacked, riddled & wracked it is the
used-uppedness at lost, at
last, heart-
lubber.

In scraggy lingo lost,
high mean-
times petering, thickets of
glitch & scrawn:
split for abysmal, hopalong
underword, head for no exit,
grapshrapnel yore spelunking.
Fractal untongue.

Hang-
heavy heart, how
crippled you venture. How
hobbled you roam. Into the wake-up and
die of it – hang-
heavy dawdler, dis-
consolate clinger: burrow & sing.

Innerly, underly: empty.
Outerly, party on.
Godloss once was a time, but now the
times devolve in the timeless mind of Mickey.
This too was human.
Noman's diaspora. Epiphanic o.

Ologies foundle. Oxies disselve.
Wordscapes and what they abstem,
neo & geo & ortho,
relics and runes:
oncelings, trekking to gack in gobi pastures,
erstlings on baffin floes.

In silicon gridlock, in
quagmeat extremis – *basta*, on wings of success,
still we snog through
sputum waste to
caramelize the Beloved,
riffle thru alley slop for a gob of awe.

Ex-
tinction warmup dues: feel the
mindmeat resist.
Pre-necro hush, bombbalm to the planet but
yip yap yip go the ostrich curs of the brain.

Bite down on un-
tology.
Nuzzle the brink of extremis.

Not tell goodbye.
Not strum farewell to sweetgrass/tundra/icecap,
nor plink so-
langsyne wackadieu to ozone eden.

No whalesong kumbaya.
Nor lynx nocturne, nor
papagayo kissoffs.
Not toll goodbye.

So much is gone, so much is
set to go.
Not peal goodbye.
No geopalinode, no solo mio.

Just,
hush for the snuffed; for
us, anathema.

Flin-
tinlyexcaliburlockjut.

Tectonic aubade.

IV

Under the
thes, under the as, under the
unders –
old folds of *other*, ob-
structing our schlep to the warm & fuzzy:

slag in the heartcraw,
paradise named away.

In cess, in dis-
ownmost, in ripture,
in slo-mo history cease,
in bio in haemo in necro – yet how
dumbfound how
dazzled, how
mortally lucky to be.

And the unredeemable names
devolve in their
liminal slouch to abyss.
I gather the crumbs of hiatus.

The blank where *evil* held.
The hole called *beholden.*

That phantom glyphs resound, that
lacunae be burnished.
That it not be leached from memory: once,
earth meant otherly.

Deathbreath of the unbeholden.
Mouth of the lorn.
Mining for syllable
rectitude, you struck clean seams of
lesser, of lesion, of
pitted implacable least.
Homefree at last in a whiteout of shock & Seine.

Because the pangs are poised to swarm the city gates.
Because it was flesh-eating crime.
Last throe of the dice, that echolalic dinger.
The earth is in shock. You must bear it.

Dieseldown momma yr mutants.
Pater in litho yr cum.
Bittybear boomp you go
woebegone/wordbegone/worldbegone
allaway home.

Lungfast in
ernity. Talisman flybys
abounding, a-
borting. And
hitherly, thitherly, *nyet*: the
nightly clips of specimen grit & torture.

Through
glittery templates of e-
merce, say cheese.
Peekaboo in the
global lobophony.
Locked pocks in the heyday of value-free, I
shush to their witness:
that evil is real.
Unassimilable. Inexpungeable. Undisownable.

In naughtsong apprentice. In no-
zone neophyte.
And the coldsweat futures collide, they
jockey for
pathophanic edge. No fore-
lore, only the
underthrum.
Only the fat-chance shitpant survival inhale.

Last call for a trashable planet,
bring it on home.
Bring it on *sotto*, bring it on
shockabye. Bring it on oil-
wise, soilwise, waterwise, methuselah –
memory holes in the phyla, and
bring it on home.

(If home still
has a home. If roots
still grope for rootedness. If
butcherama,
botcherama, wide-screen
world has not yet
metamulched what is.)

And farfew the habitat heroes,
bring it on AWOL.
Bring it on oilwork, soilwork, patchwork, be-
gin again – through
plagues of our fathers, blue
culpa.   And
bring it on, bring it on home.

V

Lost word in the
green going down,
husk of a logos,
crybaby word, out
dragging your passel of absence –
little word lost, why in the
demeaninged world would I
cradle your lonely?
You, little murderer? You, little cannibal dreg?!

And are creatures of
nothing.
I noth you noth we
long have we nothed we
shall noth, staunch in true
nothing we
noth in extremis, noth until
habitat heartstead green galore & species
relinquish the terrene ghosthold;
crumble to alphadud; stutter to rumours of *ing.*

Trolling for gravitas.
Sussing the parsecs, dowsing for
day-one *tremendum* – sizzle of
is in the thoughtsong.
                                        And you
too, if possessed: luck-
lock into pingdots anonymous. You too, my
farhither posse –
exceed me; excel me.
Through droughts & ghost savannas,
don't let me founder.
Through critterly whiteouts, compadres –
                                                            with your giddyup
inkles of tecto-extremis; your urches, your
fewfuls of penance & laud.

Plea pleading, pretty-
please pleadings.

By rupture to open: shock of
creature/no creature; first
barrow first gonesong first memory lingo freight.
Euphrates and Nile.
First harvest first parchment retention; first
pogrom obsolute.
First lost & last.

Plea pleading: that
all my truths be false.

Wordward, on mission, remiss.
Dime-
store dexterity, jittery praise –
lipsynching awe all the way to the grave of the unknown onus:
memory stutter; one smidgen, one scantling of thank.

Was a one, was a
once, was a nothing:
mattered and gone. And how cleanly

our *floruit* will fade into
moteflicker, starcycle, eddies of
gloryfit ex. Where

nothing will
sing of us; build on us; blazon our
hubris & only

You who.
You who never, who
neverest, who
ever unart.
You who summon the watch, who
hamstring the seeker, you who piss in the wine:
with this jawbone this raga this entrail,
with this pyrrhic skiptrace.
You who egg, who
slag, who un, who

Lullabye wept as asia
buckled,
rockabye einstein and all.

One for indigenous,
two for goodbye,
adam and eve and dodo.

Fly away mecca,
fly away rome,
lullabye wept in the lonely.

Once the iguanodon,
once the U.N.,
hush little orbiting gone.

Blind
light, blind
night, blind blinkers.
Blind of the lakelorn/of
lumpen/the scree.
In terminal ought and deny, indelible isprints.
Palping the scandalscript. Sniffing the
petrified *fiat*.

Stone uppance.
Starspunk shivaree.

Conjoin me.

YESNO

Song sinister. Song
ligature:
sing counter.
Are there honks, are there glyphs, are there
bare alingual grunts that
tonguefastly cleave to the iflift of
habitat mending? the judder of unsong un-
sung?

VI

If it walks like apocalypse. If it
squawks like armageddon.
If stalks the earth like anaphylactic parturition.
If halo jams like septicemic laurels, if
species recuse recuse if mutti clearcut, if
earth remembers how & then for good forgets.
If it glows like neural plague if it grins, if it
walks like apocalypse –

Blah-blah was easy, we
diddled the scrutable chunks;
whole hog was beyond us.

Bugspace &
chugspace ahead,
welcome wormlandia.

The birds con-
trive a nest. The wolves a lair.
Sheer matricide is rare.

Undernot rising. Bad
OM, the
holes in the wholly.

Bottleneck countdown; logomelt
cri du corps.
Stuck ruckus of geodilations.

What foetal botch impends? What
natal *awk*?
What gene-flubbed
cargo from postmark netherly?

Walk soft, conquistador. Among your
teeming climes and species,
bwana, beware. No
brook is what it seems, nor
veldt, nor pampas.

Sahib, go slow,
tread light in the food-chain.
The cattle tick, the trout betray; sur-
veille the very air,
it stinks of ambush.

Bwana get back, the
stats are leaking!
Inside the palisade, chop-
chop your ownmost DNA is
flaunting injun spin.

And kiss yourselves goodbye.
Is pasha crash, is
genghis melt is
its of you defecting.
No shelter. *Pasaran.*

Hope, you illicit
imperative, throw me a bone.
What sump, what gunge, what
sputter of itsy renewal?
What short shot
skitter of green reprise?

Combing the geo-pre-
frontal, scritch-
scratching for relicts of *yes*.

Giddyup, ganglia.

Skulldug, with sonic contusions.
Hushhammer riffs.

Still singable
coleoptera. Still ozone
ave, still
redwoods memorious: earth

clamant, earth
keening earth
urnal, earth
gravid with loss.

Fluke
crusoe on boolean
sands, heart-
stopt with elderlore – still

spackled with
plosions of
let-there-be. *In-*
cipit afterplanet.

Here's to destiny chumps for a change.
Rogue arthurs; geek
parsifals; flammable joans of *salut*. To
stumblebum gandhis.

Who but a bupkus
quixote would tilt at the corporate mindmills?
Who but a blunderling
underling hoot at the emperor's shanks?

Homeheart, great loanheart,
hang in;
blue planet, hold on.

Are scouts of the aquifer perilous –
ownheart, hang in.
Marsh templars. Heroes of tall grass resumption;
geodyssey samurai.

Not fold, great homeheart,
hang in.
Hold hard in the septiclot thromb of extremis.

And noful the species lacunae the alphazed shambles,
but yesward the clearwater improv & biogrit slog,
and noful the corporate borgias the aquagoth vaders,
but yesward the stewards emergent in homewhether stab,
and noful chromutant the decibel swoosh of warmwarning,
but yesward the jiminy wakeup to planetude lost –
and noful-but-yesward the herenow & bountyzip nowhere.

VII

Shucking our way to
us, in the crannies of impasse:
tarbaby toughlove.

Sloughing the fossilfix,
kicking the oink of the oil.

Nobody owns us. Nobody
owes us. Pork riddance.

Oofage & offage &
downboy.
Gravity prod.

Dream on – of
bambino returning,
pox abated,
of scarified urchin-come-home.

Dream-on of bambino regained.
Wildward the
clearcut, oceans umbilical,
ozone declension on hold.

Bambino bambino, in
toxiholic recoil.
Escapist sanities.
Dreamfast, or nought.

As if a day more
diurnal, a night more
maternal, a planet more
chockful of plenum & wonders still dawdled ex
mammary/machina/magica,
poised for a last-real comeback.

And it falls like rain.
And it signifies like plague of indigenous nada.
And sluffs the everlocal yoke of *is*, while
gaga savants plot prosthetic fixes,
and noli tangos glide the lie fantastic, and
debit, debit, debit moans the moon –

telling how speakspace
puckers. How it
swivels and clots & ka-
boom! Percur-
vations in meanfield. Skewed
mentrics. Bunched losswaves. Impromptible knots of rebeing.
Rosetta palaver, unclued.

Cold kaddish. In majuscule winter,
whistle down dixie to dusk;
coho with agave to dust.

Bison with orca commingled –
whistle down dixie. With
condor to audubon dust.

52 pickup, the species.
Beothuk, manatee, ash:
whistledown emu.

Vireo, mussel, verbena – cry
bygones, from heyday to dusk.
All whistling down dixie to dust.

Pitch lumen. Crag
nadir. Sag tor.

Old icons go blank on the
dial, and the cumulo litter of *was*
exfoliates,
oliates,
oompahs the local to pulver.

How hew to the
pushpull? How
straddle the twain of what is?

How surd a blurward stut. How
peewee thingsong,
surfing the plenary killcurve.

Barbary whoopup;
snatches of contact *ave*.

And borbo of cacahosanna: of smew of
beluga of animavegetal pibroch –
mixmuster of raggedy allsorts, syl-
labic in habitat soup.

Gumbo of
arkitude flotsam.
Flicker of
legacy toddlers, of
oldsoul avatar orphans.

Earth, you almost enough.
Hoof-high to excelsis, trilobite
sutra, cordillera jackpot:

into the new of attrition, the
birth of the lopped.
Into biosaudades.

Too fell a fate, green-
gone inheritor;
iotacome donner & ooze – still singing,

Hail to the unextinct,
oomph to the lorn-being-born.

Mid-
mortem the greenly; mid-
greening the renaissant thud –
mixmatrix our motherland.

Grammars of outcome,
twin-
twined in collision/collusion.

In plenody, threnody, whenody,
snatches of
gracemare.

Bipsychopathways.
Ontonot denizen splat.

No DNA for the crunch – we got
neural nothing.
No yesno receptors; no template for cosmochaos.
No filter for earthly redamption.

Make me
cortical skootch in the trackless.
Amygdala vamp.

Sing me
synapse of hap and despire.

VIII

What can, cog-
nostic with earthwrack, be
(who?ishly) known to co-
here, co-now with the
ratiosacral flex of
original yes?

Whacked grammar of terra
cognita. Old lingo
aphasic, nuworldspeak mute
mutant mutandis –
fumbumbling what
aleph? whose googoo? which syllab? Test-living what
schizoparse of *am*?

High whys of
lossolalia,
one blurt at a time.

Wildword the bounty extant.

Is earthscan in biscript, is
doublespeak goners-&-*hail*. Still itching to

parse with a two-tongued heart, shambala
scrapings. To
praise with a broken art.

There is a fuse. A fuss. A flex of intent:
subsingular *is* on the hoof.
Radical larrup & given.

And it whiches, it
eachly enjoins.
Old dolittle spate.

To mark it, to
mark its incessance is
riteful as breathbone.

Halebent for
origin.
Creaturely mooch in the means.

And avian farewells:
wordless in blinkerblank.
And nematode roads silting under:
hushmost palabras.
Cling to reverable, clang of no alibi, scrawk of un
uttered.
Of umbryo dicta, synching the lock-
jaw: [ ].

Ace of my heart, a-
hoy!   Don't let me founder.
Glottis of varmints & *uh-oh*.
Sentry of parlous locales.

Blue who of bad corners,
wreckabye trekster – gone
geistmates. My
no-show amigos:

don't bail on me now.

Crashable brainscape: not
crash. Exo-
skeletal whir of controls. Of
controls! Of skidlock, of some-
body-stop-us.

By pinsteps to choreocrackup.
Vertigo yen.

Courting the
glitch in the hominid regnum; craving slop-
stoppage of clash & blurn.

As stuttle inflex the genomes.
As bounty floundles.
As coldcock amnesia snakes thru
shoreline/sporelane/syngone –
hi diddle

template, unning become us,
palimpsest gibber & newly.

I spin the yin stochastic, probble a
engram luff, & parse haw
bareback the whichwake, besoddle a thrashold flux.

Calling all
lords of the rigamort tango,
maestros of entropy glide:
we're pushing it
to with an amazon shimmy, hoofing it
fro with a greenhouse fandango; little bit
closer with canopy kissoffs, little bit
farther with coral abrasions –

Stepping lightly, cortex courageous,
high-hats macabre: keep keep keep
pumping that critterly whiteout, goosing it
faster in biophobe boogie;
doing the
gainful extinctions con carny, towing them
bones in the geospazz conga –

Last call for the
champs of demise now:
one more
glug of that sweet intifada, one more

slug of the rictus merengue;
treading the
rockabye samba to notown, strutting the
kamikaze victory obit –

Bellyful:
burnout is
best.

IX

Baby come back. Come
easy come queasy come faraway-willaway,
bonehead electric like big boys but
baby come back, breathe
deep in the motherlode. Dumb
kopf in a sling & come broken,
baby come home.

You fold you are
folded, late-breaking primate, and
brought to who-knew.
Fold you are
null again, nil again, knell again – one-swat no-
see-um & whose.
Stud of no
throne no dominion, kingshit of doodly.
Frag in the mean of let-be.

Earth heres, earth
nows, is there
nothing?

What whats?
Inlisten.
What quickens?

Inner than
polipulse, homer than breathbeat, listen to
isten. To

istence. Listen to *inguish*. Listen to
is.

Deep
is, and be
struck. Be stricken.
Be amnioflex of the daily, as
things wriggle free of their names,
subsist in
sheer diggity *fiat.*

Be wild & be-
wildered.
Undermilk arbour, arbourmilk under –
sesame endwise:
stillwill and re-boot.
Squiggles of *ing* on a
field of native null.

Herk lurch to
protobang –
quotidi-/
aeonic aḥ-
ha! What comes
to be is
beholden.

Was HIGGS; was BANG; was URBOP. Was
max in a smidgen. Was *IS*.
Googols of firstforce. Itch rhythming –

still rampant in lichen & esker,
aphid & tanager. Still
startup in coral & smee.

Gimpalong beauties. Fucked
fractals of ogeny sprong.

What we sniff/palp/schmeck/wrack/
ravish, but
can't commandeer. The
plosive being of beings.
Quickquark the ammonite, cognate the andes;
gratuitous stakeouts in time. Each a
fleck of first-day durance, a
fluxy reverb,
sheer chronojolt & onwards.

Thrum of material kickstart.
Jiggers of genesis.

Hope without
bandwidth.
Itch without mouth.
Deepsong gone long-gone, gone not-yet to ground in a
flurry of *shhh*.

Newful the needful – re-
boreal peeps in kaputski.
No north, no south, just yenway.
Just, hunkerdownduly & looselip a blurt of begin.

Which thing is us.
We of the
waste-deep the
westering, we of the
cackabye outstinct on ice.

And are bodily implicates.
Are denizen-drenched, self-x'd,
are phyxiate foundlings,
woozy with birthright and
laced with caterwaul *rerum*.

Clamber down babel, climb down to the
nearaway country of homewhere. Of
bastard belong.

At the still open grave of the
not-yet-write-
offable cashcorpse –
blindblabbing our
gobshut, our
gutted-by-greenslag, our undisad-
missible burden: *for-*
gi-   *forgi-*

In morituri funk.

Body of primal, body of
plumb: it is to
you we owe our being,
carne of undergone epochs.

Destructible mother, survive us,
widewinnow our folly.
Foregather, in interlore
rehab agon, our
little, our lustral, our late.

X

Of more the less; of
least, prognostipangs.
Scrabbling for *abc.*

No heaven, no
beanstalk, bare earth.

Shedding what pyrotech-
tactics?
Threading what speakab/un-
speakable, ekable, seekable
gauntlet of need?

Terragon tilth, or
heartwork in kinderpolis.
To couch in the knit of the sinew, to
ponder refoliant scrub.
To gawp at what thrives without us.
To jimmy the civil equations, resetting for
osteo clicks of alignment,
onus upon us;
salaam to what heals
in the real.

Extempore if-
space & greening,
plant heartflag here.

Thru witslog, thru willslog to
glimmers of thingdom come;
pitch soulhold here.

Labour & claimstead – of
inchables,
karma oscura.

Staking the bundle. Brought,
broke, to
indigenous *fiat*.

Squeaks from the sisyphus chorus.
Hums from the crunch.
Dopey & grumpy & doc, just
truckin along –
here come chorale;
mind to the
grindstone, ear to the plough.

Hi-
hoein along with a song:
What home but here? Whose grubby paws but ours?

With a *yes*, with a *no*, with a
yesno;
sonics in simuljam.

To habitate crossbeing.
To ride both reals at once. To least-
wise stay
vif in detritus/un-
lulled by the blessingbait green.

If inly, if only, if
unly: heart-
iculate improv,
sussing the emes of what is.

Nor hunker in losslore, nor
kneejerk abracadaver.

Cripcryptic rejuice! Ec-
statisyllabic largesse –
rekenning, rekeening, re-
meaning our wordly demesne.

Grunts from the trench, the killzone:
peeps from the front.

Lithoslag/bioslag/noöslag –
hasta la omega.

Ciao to the caesarly, bye to the kaiserly, howdy
grim repo.

Hemis of brokensole. Demis. Mutt
angelus minims.

If hope disorders words, let
here be where.
Lingotectonics. Gondwana nar-
ruption vocale.

How can the
tonguetide of object/sub-
jection not garble what pulses in
isbelly?

Nearflung & thingmost, re-
tuit sheer carnival logos. Where
nouns ignite
moves in the dance they denote:
moniker lifelines.
Cedarfast. Willowpang. Maplemind.
Oakable homing, notched in the bone.

Only co-
phonic. Co-
founded. Cofoundered.
Only galore.

Mercator cleanup or what?
Toxijam loosened, slum-
praxis goosed;
techmate relievo or what.

Alphas of stricken, bare omega noodlers –
swot to revivify human,
vamping on taptoes of *must*.

By the law by the lab by the ballot:
sanity sweat.
Lost-ditch endorphins or what.
Hometruth cojones. Or what?

Tell me, tall-
tell me a tale. The one about
starless & steerless & pinch-me, the
one about unnable now – which they did-did-
did in the plume of our pride, and
could not find the way home.
Little perps lost.

Yet a rescue appeared, in the
story a saviour arose. Called
limits. Called
duedate, called countdown ex-
tinction/collide. Called, eyeball to ego:
hubris agonistes.

Bad *abba* the endgame. In-
seminal doomdom alert:
pueblo naturans, or
else. But the breadcrumbs are gone, and the
story goes on, and how
haply an ending no
nextwise has shown us, nor known.

Dennis Lee has written more than twenty books of poetry, including *Un* and *Yesno*, the predecessors to *Testament*. His *Civil Elegies* won the Governor General's Literary Award, and his children's poetry is read around the world. He is also a noted essayist, song lyricist, and editor, and was the co-founder of Anansi in 1967. He is currently a resident artist at Toronto's Young Centre, the home of Soulpepper Theatre.

¶ *Testament* was edited for the press by Don McKay. Thanks also to Gordon Teskey.

The typography and design are based on Robert Bringhurst's template for *Un*, and the type was set by Sari Naworynski. The typeface is Van den Keere, a digital text family produced in the 1990s by Frank Blokland at the Dutch Type Library in The Hague. The roman is based on the work of the Flemish punchcutter Hendrik van den Keere (c.1540-1580), and the italic is the work of his French-born colleague François Guyot (c. 1510-1570).

The author photo is by Susan Perly.